Gathered and Preserved

By Suzanne L. Flynt, Susan McGowan
and Amelia F. Miller

Memorial Hall
Pocumtuck Valley Memorial Association
Deerfield, Massachusetts

The Pocumtuck Valley Memorial Association
dedicates this Memorial Hall guide book to
Russ Arthur Miller
1914-1988
Longtime friend of PVMA and President 1971-1985

Only a visit to Memorial Hall in Deerfield, Massachusetts, can bring to life the depth and scope of the extensive and eclectic collection of the Pocumtuck Valley Memorial Association (PVMA), begun in 1870. An introductory guide can at best merely suggest the quality and variety of the collection, but must inevitably fail to demonstrate the quantity. Objects included in this book have been selected for their intrinsic value, wide appeal, and historical significance, but the initial collection, gathered and preserved by George Sheldon, Deerfield historian and founder of PVMA, illustrates the spirit of the Victorian Age — if one iron pot was good, ten were better. At Memorial Hall the same may be said of cradles, chests, tools, textiles, paintings, Indian artifacts, ceramics, glassware, architectural fragments, and all articles related to the lives of former residents of Deerfield and of the surrounding area, once occupied by the Pocumtuck Indians.

Another of Sheldon's early concepts, his initial "memorial" approach, is responsible for the collection's present major strength. He accessioned each article as a memorial to a particular local family and frequently documented the entry with a detailed family history. As a result, the provenance of everyday household objects as well as important artistic pieces is known. PVMA's collection is notable for its indepth and specific documentation, offering the visitor an authentic cultural picture of this Connecticut River Valley region and providing scholars with an unsurpassed source for research.

The degree of Sheldon's documentation has frequently determined choices for this guide to Memorial Hall which attempts to convey the diversity of PVMA's collection by juxtaposing objects of artistic and historic merit with those of a more humble nature. Valued for a variety of reasons — fine craftsmanship, rarity, association with a particular event in history, or illustrative of the breadth of George Sheldon's vision — all objects in Memorial Hall tell a story. This guide represents an effort to balance Sheldon's view of his amassed "Relics and Curiosities," the roots of the collection, with a late-twentieth-century appreciation for the refinements and common tools of daily life in the past.

Timothy C. Neumann,
Executive Director

1. ALLEN SISTERS PHOTOGRAPH, Deerfield, 1914.

This photograph, a carefully staged scene complete with ''colonial'' clothing, is characteristic of the romanticized view of the past offered by the Deerfield sisters Frances S. Allen (1854-1941) and Mary E. Allen (1858-1941) in the late nineteenth and early twentieth centuries. The impact of the colonial revival with reminders of the nation's past was strongly felt in Deerfield. Crafts of earlier years were revived, and Memorial Hall Museum was dedicated to preserve and to exhibit relics and curiosities from Deerfield and the surrounding Franklin County. Residents here, similar to many in the nation, were looking backward to what seemed a happier, less harried, and more prosperous time — an ideal New England which they longed to recapture.

PVMA Founded

The Pocumtuck Valley Memorial Association (PVMA) was founded in Deerfield as just that — a memorial association. Yet the early concept was modest. As several men gathered by chance on a street corner in nearby Greenfield in 1869, they recalled a tragic event in the history of Deerfield: the surprise attack by French and Indians from Canada on the stockaded outpost shortly before dawn on February 29, 1704. Laying waste the town, the enemy then gathered together surviving men, women, and children, and leaving behind the smouldering ruins of settlers' homes all began a three-hundred-mile march through deep snow to Canada.

Of the captives, numbering about 104, many would fall along the way and one of the first was Eunice Williams, wife of Deerfield's minister, the Reverend John Williams. On January 15, Eunice had given birth to her eleventh child, Jerusha, and on March 1, Eunice, failing to keep up with her captors, was killed near the Green River some eight miles north of Deerfield. There in Greenfield on the street corner in 1869 the conversants resolved to commemorate Eunice Williams and her tragic death by placing a stone marker near the site where she had fallen.

Out of this conversation in Greenfield grew within a year the intention to form an association to pay tribute to all early settlers — the Pocumtuck Indians as well as those who followed — and the first meeting of PVMA took place in a crowded Deerfield Town Hall on May 26, 1870. Article 1 of the original constitution stated the new association's object:

> . . .collecting and preserving such memorials, books, papers and curiosities as may tend to illustrate and perpetuate the history of the early settlers of this region, and of the race which vanished before them; and the erection of a memorial hall in which such collections can be securely deposited.

Six years before the Philadelphia Centennial of 1876 gave rise to a national awareness of the past and the ensuing establishment of many historical societies in New England, the PVMA was planned, organized, and chartered. When the stone was ultimately dedicated to Eunice Williams on August 12, 1884, it bore the inscription "Erected by P.V.M.A."

Memorial Hall

As residents of Deerfield and neighboring towns

2. ALLEN SISTERS PHOTOGRAPH, "MONUMENT TO THE BARS FIGHT," Deerfield, c. 1903.

When, in the early 1870s, the idea for a Memorial Hall was born, the proposal also included a plan to commemorate "with some simple memorial" those residents of the county slain while attempting to establish the frontier settlement. The site where Eunice Williams fell on February 29, 1704, was marked by the PVMA in 1884, and about 1901, Miss C. Alice Baker provided a sandstone monument to top a grassy mound in the old Albany Road burying ground in recognition of forty-eight men, women, and children who lost their lives in the 1704 massacre. At a PVMA Field Meeting at the Bars settlement south of the village street, a boulder was dedicated in honor of Samuel Allen in July 1903. Allen, who "stood his ground while his children fled," was slain in August 1746, along with four of his neighbors while gathering hay in a field near his home. The assault, by a small detachment from the army who had captured Fort Massachusetts (near the present Williamstown, Massachusetts) five days earlier, constituted the last Indian attack in Deerfield.

Pocumtuck Memorial Hall.
PERSPECTIVE VIEW.

*3. LITHOGRAPH OF "POCUMTUCK MEMORIAL HALL,"
Deerfield, c. 1876.*

*This presentation drawing was submitted to PVMA by a now
unidentifield architect about 1876. The intent to build a hall
to house and to exhibit local relics, manuscripts, and the Old
Indian House door on land purchased for the purpose by
George Sheldon, never materialized. Sheldon had bought
land facing the common, and had moved the old Ware Store
building then standing on it. In 1877, the trustees of Deerfield
Academy offered their brick building with one and about
three-quarters of an acre of land to PVMA for $2000 plus
"PVMA's estate on the old Ware Corner."*

began to search their attics, their barns, and the fields
they plowed for relics of the past in the spirit of con-
tributing to the rapidly growing PVMA collection, the
need for a place to exhibit the collection also grew. In
1875 a small lot west of the common was made
available for a proposed museum building, tentatively
called "Pocumtuck Memorial Hall." Efforts to raise
funds for the building were mounted, stressing the need
to make accessible the collections then scattered in
private homes. In 1876 a committee reported its recom-
mendation that the building be brick and fire-resistant
throughout, and a now unidentified architect submitted
a "Perspective view."

While the appeal was underway, the Trustees of
Dickinson High School and Deerfield Academy an-
nounced plans for a new school building facing the
Deerfield common. All plans for the Pocumtuck
Memorial Hall were set aside when on December 31,
1877, the Trustees sold to PVMA their original building
designed by Asher Benjamin and erected in 1797-1798.
Shortly thereafter the Academy moved to the center of

town and occupied in part the site of the proposed
Pocumtuck Memorial Hall.

Converting the old three-story brick Academy into a
museum required alterations and renovations. Among
these were heightening the third floor by three feet,
replacing old wood shingles with a new tin roof, remov-
ing third floor partitions, and covering the exterior with
a coat of red paint. By the late fall of 1879, work was
sufficiently completed for the building to receive
PVMA's collection and for it to be arranged in newly
completed cases.

Although the house of John Sheldon, built in 1699,
had survived the 1704 massacre, it would not survive
the nineteenth century. On May 30, 1848, the legendary
Old Indian House, home of the Hoyt family since 1744,
was demolished, but its battered door, with an assort-
ment of less auspicious architectural details, was saved.

*4. OLD INDIAN HOUSE DOOR, from the Ensign John Sheldon
House, Deerfield, 1699.*

*When John Sheldon built a house within the stockade at the
north end of Deerfield's common or training ground in 1699,
his house was reputed to have been the largest in town. Its
heavy, laminated front door is composed of two layers of
pine boards fastened together with rosehead nails applied in
a diamond pattern; the exterior boards are vertical and the
interior ones horizontal. The door retains the hole and gashes
made by the French and Indian attackers on the night of
February 29, 1704. The story of that night has been repeated
often: ". . .the stout door. . .resisted the efforts to break it
down. It was cut partly through with axes, and bullets were
fired through the place at random, one of which killed Mrs.
[Hannah] Sheldon as she was sitting on a bed in the east
room."*

*Despite attempts in 1847 to save the old Sheldon house,
now recognized as one of America's first efforts in historic
preservation, the house was pulled down on May 30, 1848. Its
scarred door with its romantic associations was saved and
became one of the earliest tourist attractions in the Connecticut River Valley. Through its presence the memory of Deerfield's massacre remained alive, helping to foster an unusual
degree of historical consciousness among residents and
visitors to the town. With the destruction of the Old Indian
House, citizens began to question the fate of the other relics of
their past; this concern eventually resulted in the formation
of the Pocumtuck Valley Memorial Association and the subse-
quent opening of its museum where the door and other
material evidence of the past could be safely housed. People
were urged to send to George Sheldon "such articles of interest they may possess." The Old Indian House door, one of
only two seventeenth-century exterior doors in existence in
America, and the most complete, has been displayed at
Memorial Hall since the opening of the museum in 1880.*

*Purchased from the Hoyt family in 1863 by Dr. Daniel
Dennison Slade of Boston; returned to Deerfield in 1868; entrusted to PVMA in 1879.*

Deerfield, Mass., Memorial Hall.

5. POSTCARD OF MEMORIAL HALL, 1910-1915.

Designed by Asher Benjamin (1773-1845), New England architect-builder, the Memorial Hall building was constructed for Deerfield Academy and was dedicated on January 1, 1799. The original two-story building had two front doors, allowing separate entrances for male and female students. A third floor was added in 1809-1810 to accommodate boarders. When the building was purchased by the Pocumtuck Valley Memorial Association in 1877, further changes were made: the bricks were painted red, the roof was raised, and metal sash were installed in all windows in an attempt to make the building fireproof. The Greenfield Gazette and Courier *noted that "the PVMA building presents quite an improved appearance...its dedication, when completed will probably be the next Deerfield sensation." Shortly after the September 8, 1880, dedication the Springfield* Republican *observed that "the unsightly appearance of what used to be the old Academy is improved so much beyond expectation that people are wondering now why somebody didn't think to make a hotel of it before the Association secured the property."*

The door, having traveled to numerous locations since 1848, found a worthy permanent home in PVMA's museum. When the museum was dedicated on September 8, 1880, visitors could read the inscription "Memorial Hall" over the front entrance, and inside, the historic door received wide attention.

George Sheldon

Born in 1818 in Deerfield, George Sheldon had participated in the 1869 street corner conversation and was certainly the leading force, if not the founder of PVMA. As PVMA's first President, an office he continued to hold until his death in 1916, and also the "Cabinet-Keeper" — a title to be replaced with that of Curator in 1882 — Sheldon oversaw the business of the Association and concentrated on the development of a collection. A farmer in his early years, he would become increasingly involved with historical matters only in the second half of his nearly century-long lifetime. At age thirty, he had witnessed the demolition in 1848 of his ancestors' home, the Old Indian House, and he later claimed that this event first awakened him to the need for preserving local history and landmarks.

As an historian, Sheldon's concerns were always to commemorate, to preserve, to collect, and to record. Those goals motivated him as he nurtured and guided PVMA, encouraging all those of his acquaintance to donate family manuscripts — letters, deeds, diaries, ac-

6. PORTRAIT OF GEORGE SHELDON (1818-1916) by Augustus Vincent Tack (1870-1949), with a selection of musical instruments.

George Sheldon was near the end of his long life when this portrait was painted by Augustus Vincent Tack. Remembered for his personal initiative, original research, and wide knowledge, Sheldon was an antiquarian, author, historian, and curator, and it was largely because of his foresight and perseverance that the museum and the library collections of PVMA were formed.

On view with Sheldon's portrait are musical instruments, including a bass viol played by Philo Munn (1813-1895) in Deerfield's Brick or Unitarian Church prior to the acquisition of an 1889 organ. The viol was made by Jeremiah Wait (1779-1855) of Whately, Massachusetts, in 1832. Made by Alpheus Babcock in Boston about 1823, the piano was owned by Edward Hitchcock (1793-1864), President of Amherst College from 1845-1854.

Portrait: Gift of Mrs. William Howe, 1977. Viol: Gift of Julia (Munn) Ashley, 1905. Piano and stool: Gifts of Andrew Hamilton, 1894.

count books, and documents of all sorts — as well as furniture, tools, paintings, ceramics, and "costumes." He was known to settle personal debts upon receiving a carved chest or a portrait which he coveted for PVMA's collection. He was as equally dedicated to PVMA's library as to antiquities and relics.

Further, as author of a vast number of historical articles, he encouraged PVMA members to research and to write about historical subjects to be read at annual meetings beginning in 1870. These were published in a series of volumes under the title of *History and Proceedings of the Pocumtuck Valley Memorial Association*. In 1895 and in 1896 his remarkable *History of Deerfield* was published in two volumes.

In 1897 at the age of seventy-eight, Sheldon married Jennie Maria Arms. Jennie, who had a considerable reputation as a natural scientist, helped her husband in his latter years and served as PVMA's Curator from 1913-1938 and as President from 1929-1938.

George and Jennie Sheldon together dominated PVMA for a period of almost seventy years. The institution became inseparably identified with their leadership and it is due to their energy and vision that Memorial Hall remains strong and vigorous well over a century after the museum opened to the public.

In hindsight the Sheldon legacy has stood up well. As one of the pioneer museum personages in America, George Sheldon helped to define what an American museum could be. The breadth, range, and quality of his collecting efforts become increasingly apparent. It would be impossible to build a collection of such astonishing documentary value today.

The Sheldons and PVMA were deeply involved in collecting and in preservation, but their commitment to education and to promoting public awareness was also significant, creating an historical aura — the source of Deerfield's present appeal and national reputation.

In his own time George Sheldon received acclaim as far more than a local historian, collector, and author. He participated in the founding of The Trustees of Public Reservations in Massachusetts, incorporated in 1891, and in 1906 he was elected a member of The Massachusetts Historical Society. In Deerfield, his vision and the life he breathed into PVMA continue to shape its standards and goals.

Early Museum

When Memorial Hall was dedicated on Wednesday, September 8, 1880, in the converted Deerfield Academy

7. ALLEN SISTERS PHOTOGRAPH, *The Colonial Kitchen, c. 1890-1900*

The room called "the colonial kitchen" illustrates the approach of PVMA's founders as they attempted to interpret the period of Deerfield's early settlement. Organized around a fireplace, itself an outsized theatrical backdrop, is a clutter of more than 800 items "where this progressive age can come and ponder over and wonder at the various utensils used in the domestic economy of 100 years ago." Even before the museum opened, the PVMA committee of arrangements had voiced its intent to set apart a room in which to exhibit an old family kitchen, qualifying the effort as a very early, perhaps the first, use of the period room concept in an American museum. By 1891, annual meetings of the Association were held in the "comfortable, ancient kitchen," with the members seating themselves "amidst the antiquities." The colonial kitchen at Memorial Hall represents a view of pioneer domesticity seen through the eyes of nineteenth-century antiquarians.

building, there were seven exhibition rooms awaiting the public. The three-story ell built by Deerfield Academy in 1810 was reserved to accommodate a caretaker. On the ground floor, to the right of the entrance, relics were displayed pertaining to the Pocumtuck Indians. The centerpiece was the renowned Old Indian House door. In the hallway the Curator placed the historic cannon believed to have been brought to Deerfield by Massachusetts Governor Jonathan Belcher in 1735 when he held a conference with the Caughnawaga and other Indian nations.

To the left of the entrance Sheldon arranged a "colonial kitchen" centered around a fireplace with an early hearthstone from Greenfield and a mantle-tree from his own house, preserved when his center chimney was removed. The surrounding clutter of utensils, all col-

lected from local homes, creates a romantic but historically inaccurate impression of a true and more sparsely furnished kitchen, but in 1880, Sheldon's pioneer attempt to display a kitchen was innovative. Believed to be the earliest extant period setting room in a museum in this country, Sheldon's "colonial kitchen" still awaits visitors to Memorial Hall.

On the second floor the east room was allocated as a place to display domestic industries, "instruments used in ancient times for the transformation of flax into cloth, and kindred implements." The middle room was set aside in 1880 for "displaying upon its walls the tablets. . .commemorating the names and fate of the first settlers."

A library of more than 2000 volumes, "of ancient books...pamphlets and writings in manuscript," occupied the second floor west room in 1880.

While Sheldon and other members of PVMA had amassed numerous books and manuscripts, the nucleus had been greatly enhanced in 1879 when remaining members of The Deerfield Social Library, founded about 1795, voted to present its approximately 850 volumes to PVMA.

In the process of repairing the old Academy building, most partitions on the third floor had been removed, leaving only two rooms, one large and one small. When the museum opened in 1880, the large room held miscellaneous articles "with a wealth of history and romance clustering about them." The small room was designed to display objects "pertaining to an old-fashioned bed room" and was in essence another period room setting.

Academy Museum

When PVMA acquired the original Deerfield Academy building on December 31, 1877, the agreement conveyed "the old museum with some minor effects in the building." Deerfield Academy's "old museum" was in fact a collection or cabinet begun in June 1797 which included such eclectic objects as: local Indian artifacts, which are particularly significant because of their early accession dates, curiosities of nature, rocks, fish and animal bones, wasps' nests, birds' nests, a tarantula's nest, a spider in amber, and wonders brought back from sailing voyages to distant lands. Items from the "N-West Coast of America," from Calcutta, from Sicily by way of Messina, from the Isle of Bourbon (near Madagascar), Java, and from South America as well as baskets,

8. ALLEN SISTERS PHOTOGRAPH, The Colonial Bedroom, c. 1890-1900.

When PVMA founders made plans to move into the original Deerfield Academy building, the council or governing board conceived of period rooms. The 1878 PVMA Proceedings *stated the intent "to set apart one room. . .for an ancient bedroom." The bedroom, with its 1810 bedstead and Gothic pillar chintz hangings, once belonging to Seth and Caroline (Stebbins) Sheldon, was, in 1880, located on the third floor in the small room west of the Main Hall. By 1886 the bedroom was located in an alcove in the Main Hall, as depicted here.*

Also shown in the photograph is a carved chest. This was the first time a now legendary "Hadley" chest was exhibited in a museum setting. George Sheldon was one of the first to recognize the intrinsic merits of these carved chests, amassing at Memorial Hall what remains today the nation's largest collection of this widely regarded style of "Pilgrim century" furniture.

moccasins, lava from Mt. Etna, a peacock feather, King Crab fish, and a stone from Rhode Island, were formerly displayed to educate early Academy scholars.

Donors to the Academy museum included numerous descendants of early settlers of Deerfield and of neighboring towns, and many notable persons and institutions. Among the latter were the painter Ralph Earl, United States Chief Justice Oliver Ellsworth, Governor James Sullivan of Massachusetts, Dartmouth College, and "The Historical Society" — The Massachusetts Historical Society, founded in 1791 and the first such society in America.

Approximately one-third of these treasures of 1797 survive in Memorial Hall, as does the original catalogue, and the Deerfield Academy Museum is now recognized to be one of the earliest established in this country.

The Tablets

Just as the founding of PVMA was an outgrowth of the 1869 resolve to mark the site where Eunice Williams

had fallen, so was the effort to secure wall tablets as a memorial to all victims of the 1704 massacre. The tablets were to be placed in the second floor middle room of Memorial Hall; a large tablet in the center would give "a brief account of the sacking of the town," but the project progressed slowly. Not until 1882 did George Sheldon report that preparations were underway. To further the cause Sheldon contacted descendants who were "invited to contribute" a family plaque, and he noted the families who had not participated, stating that for some there were no known descendants. It had been determined that the tablets were to be of marble, and accordingly, A.A. Rankin of Greenfield and his assistant, one Mr. Monnier, were employed to cut and to carve the tablets. Finally, in 1883 at the annual meeting Sheldon reported,

> The great work of the year has been placing tablets in memory of the sufferers of February 29, 1704 in Memorial Room. . .We can now properly call this building a Memorial Hall....

9. OBJECTS FROM THE DEERFIELD ACADEMY MUSEUM.

Palm leaf fans, an image in alabaster, spoons made from Alaskan mountain goat horns, a grass cup from Alaska, and an Indian war club are among some of the curiosities from the Deerfield Academy Museum, begun in June of 1797 and transferred to PVMA in 1877. The Academy Museum was filled with objects intended to stimulate the imagination and curiosity of the pupils. Some of the items were wildly exotic, but others — "soil from about 225 historic places" accompanied by a list of those places, collections of birds' eggs and nests, fossil footprints— were more linked to the study of natural history. The collection of specimens of Franklin County minerals and compound rocks, gathered by two Deerfield men, Edward Hitchcock (1793-1864), educator and geologist, and Dr. Stephen West Williams (1790-1855), physician, beginning in 1817, was an important addition to the museum. More than 300 objects from the Academy Museum survive in Memorial Hall.

Deerfield Academy Museum; transferred to PVMA in 1877.

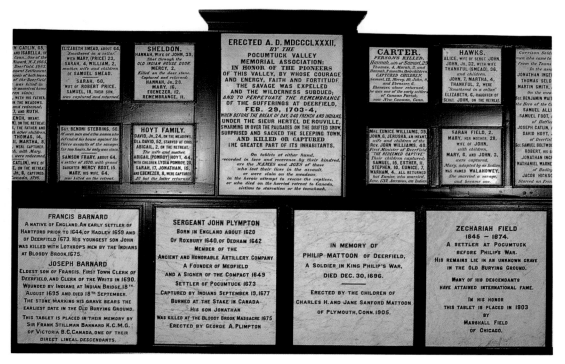

10. MEMORIAL ROOM, *Memorial Hall Museum, Deerfield.*

Marble tablets commemorate the killed and captured from the French and Indian assault on Deerfield before dawn on February 29, 1704. One of the original purposes in the formation of the museum was PVMA's intent "when enough money was raised" to place tablets in one of the rooms "bearing the names of those slain by the Indians." The project was well on its way to completion three years after the opening of the Hall in 1880, and George Sheldon reported at the 1883 annual meeting ". . .we can now properly call this building a Memorial Hall."

The Museum Grows

Beginning in 1900, PVMA yearly reports began to note the need for additional space for display and for the library. The solution was provided by Mrs. Jennie M. Arms Sheldon who in 1902 had a cottage built on PVMA grounds to create new living quarters for the custodian, who had previously lived in the 1810 north wing. From 1903 to 1905 the now evacuated wing underwent repairs and gradually began to receive the overflow. The third floor primitive bedchamber was moved into the wing, where a library annex was also established. In 1912 the library expanded when Deerfield Academy entrusted 447 volumes, mostly the remains of the original Academy library, to PVMA's keeping.

By 1915 lack of space was again a concern, and once more George and Jennie Sheldon came forward as generous benefactors when they donated a new three-story fireproof wing. The first floor of the new 1916 wing became a Colonial and Revolutionary Room. Mrs. Sheldon, after her husband's death, personally oversaw the installation of the library, now numbering nearly 20,000 books and pamphlets, on the second floor in newly built cases. The third floor was reserved for PVMA's extensive picture, map, and manuscript collection.

Uncertain Times

Jennie Sheldon's death in 1938 broke the continuity of Sheldon family leadership of PVMA. Within a year the war in Europe would begin in Poland. Effects of the war were felt by PVMA only after Pearl Harbor on December 7, 1941, when Americans, in wholehearted support of fighting forces overseas, sought means to aid the war effort on the home front. Attention turned to volunteer jobs — Civilian Defense, the Draft Board, the Red Cross.

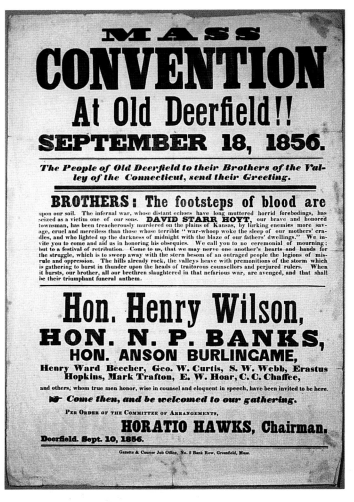

11. BROADSIDE, published by the Gazette and Courier Job Office, Greenfield, Massachusetts, 1856.

The PVMA library contains printed books, manuscripts, photographs, broadsides, and other related material gathered largely from local sources. Much of the library collection was formed between the time of the Association's founding in 1870 and the death of its principal founder, George Sheldon, in 1916, thereby representing to an extraordinary degree the life and thought of one small New England town from the close of the seventeenth century to the opening of the twentieth.

Broadsides, sheets of paper printed on one side, frequently publicized a controversy or an official proclamation, and were posted in public places. This particular notice announced, as forthcoming speakers in Deerfield, the politicians Wilson and Banks, who were outspoken in their opposition to the Kansas-Nebraska bill. David Starr Hoyt, whose name is prominent on the broadside, was a native of Deerfield. His death in 1856 during the "bloody Kansas" crisis shocked local residents who received word that Hoyt was reported murdered by pro-slavery "Border Ruffians."

Enthusiasm for Sheldon's museum waned. Wartime restrictions also took their toll on PVMA. Gas rationing caused attendance at Memorial Hall to decline; the paper shortage delayed printing of the *Proceedings;* food rationing prevented holding the traditional annual dinners. Memorial Hall was eventually closed, reopening only in 1947 on a limited basis — by appointment only.

PVMA Reopened

When in 1949 Henry N. Flynt of Greenwich, Connecticut, became President of PVMA and Helen Geier Flynt, his wife, began to serve as Councillor, the Association once again flourished. Their interest in Deerfield had begun as Deerfield Academy parents in the late 1930s and expanded when Henry Flynt was appointed President of the Academy's trustees. Becoming increasingly attracted to the town and its history, the Flynts began to restore many of the early houses along Deerfield's street and were also inevitably drawn to Memorial Hall. With the enthusiasm and support of the Flynts, PVMA membership increased, and the Publishing Committee commenced an active program reprinting works long unavailable. Annual dinners served at Deerfield Academy, with imaginative programs conceived by the Flynts, were well attended events.

PVMA 1968 - 1970

The year 1968 brought a new crisis. Memorial Hall, particularly the 1810 wing, was found to be structurally unsound. Only by closing the museum for two years could extensive and costly reconstruction and restoration be accomplished. When reopened in 1970, the museum gained new floor space. To the east of Memorial Hall the Flynts oversaw the building of a new library modeled in design after the original Academy, and PVMA's collection of books and manuscripts was moved onto the second floor thus providing space on two floors of the 1916 fireproof wing for new acquisitions, for seasonal exhibits, and for storage. Under the supervision of the Librarian, experienced personnel began to catalogue the PVMA manuscripts, thereby enhancing their availability to historians and to students.

The PVMA and Memorial Hall since 1970

Under the leadership of Russ A. Miller, who succeeded

Henry N. Flynt as President in 1971, the organization became increasingly more professional. Russ Miller's committment to the town of Deerfield began in the fall of 1928 when he entered Deerfield Academy as a freshman. In 1937 he joined the faculty at the Academy, beginning a distinguished career which lasted fifty-four years. In 1949 Russ Miller became a member of the PVMA. Thereafter, he served as a member of the Council from 1961-1988, as Vice-President from 1968-1970, and as President from 1971-1986.

With even greater emphasis on education and publishing, the museum has planned expanded programs for the membership and for the general public. Cataloguing, labeling, conserving, and rearranging the collection has continued as important donations have been received and new items purchased. Special exhibits with accompanying catalogues have found wide appeal.

The Collection

What sets Memorial Hall apart from many historical museums around the country is the extraordinary documentation and historical provenance surrounding its collection. Memorial Hall is a museum with a collection associated with dozens of specific individuals from Deerfield and nearby towns. Further, the collection is neither static nor frozen, but continues to grow as items with local and family histories become available.

12. PHOTOGRAPH OF MEMORIAL HALL, Deerfield, 1985.

Designed by Asher Benjamin and dedicated on January 1, 1799, the original brick building of Deerfield Academy became the property of PVMA on December 31, 1877. When opened to the public on September 8, 1880, as PVMA's Memorial Hall, the old Academy held George Sheldon's accumulated relics, and has ever since been home to the expanding PVMA collection. Sheldon paid tribute to the three-story building when he declared it one of PVMA's most valuable ''relics'' and in an 1886 catalogue for Memorial Hall, Luther J.B. Lincoln (1851-1902) of Deerfield recognized the appropriate new role of the old Academy,

> *It is peculiarly fitting that this old structure, whose halls have been the* alma mater *of so many past and present generations, should finally shelter these hallowed memorials of our forefathers; for it is, in itself, a monument of their farseeing and conscientious regard for the education of posterity.*

13. STONE CONTAINER, found in Bernardston, Massachusetts, late-Archaic period, c. 0-2000 B.C.; **PESTLE** and **CERAMIC VESSEL** found in Deerfield, probably late-Woodland-Contact period, c. 1000-1700 A.D.

While most prehistoric Indian artifacts in Memorial Hall are projectile points, locally found stone bowls, pestles, and ground stone tools are also represented in the collection. Pestles were used to grind plant material, and pottery objects were for storage and cooking. The ceramic vessel was found on the homelot of George Sheldon in 1871.

Stone container: Gift of Jonathan Johnson, before 1886. Pestle: Donor unknown. Ceramic vessel: Gift of George Sheldon, before 1886.

14. TOBACCO POUCH, probably Caughnawaga Mohawk, Quebec, Canada, c. 1700-1750.

The cultivation and smoking of tobacco was prevalent among male Indians of the Woodland period as early as 1000 A.D. This tobacco bag or pouch was hung from the belt or the neck.

Gift to Deerfield Academy Museum; transferred to PVMA in 1877.

15. SASHES, probably Caughnawaga Mohawk, Quebec, Canada, c. 1700 - 1750.

These sashes, typical examples of the period, were decorated with crewel wool and with glass beads, both items of English trade goods.

Upper sash: Gift to Deerfield Academy Museum by heirs of the Reverend Stephen Williams (1693-1782), who was taken captive in the 1704 Deerfield massacre, before 1799; transferred to PVMA in 1877. Lower sash: Donor unknown.

16. SHAMAN'S RATTLE, Caughnawaga Mohawk, Quebec, Canada, c. 1710-1750.

The shaman, a religious leader within a tribe, was believed to possess spiritual powers both to heal the sick and to control the future. When shaken, this ornamental otter skin, complete with skull and claws and embellished with tin bells, added drama to his rituals.
   Deerfield Academy Museum; transferred to PVMA in 1877.

17. CANOE MODEL, made by Micmac Indians, probably eastern Canada, c. 1750-1800.

The birch bark canoe is incised with double curve motifs commonly used by the Micmac tribe. These coastal Indians lived in what are now known as the Maritime Provinces: Nova Scotia, Cape Breton Island, Prince Edward Island, and the eastern shore of New Brunswick, and also in northern Maine. In 1796, the donor, James Sullivan (1744-1808), was appointed United States agent to the Halifax commission to determine the disputed boundary line of Maine. Sullivan's travels gave him ample opportunity to acquire this canoe. Sullivan, a powerful politician, was elected Governor of Massachusetts in 1807 and 1808.
   Gift of James Sullivan to Deerfield Academy Museum before 1800; transferred to PVMA in 1877.

18. PRISONER HALTER, Caughnawaga Mohawk, Quebec, Canada, 1746.

Dorothy (Williams) Ashley (1713-1808), wife of the Reverend Jonathan Ashley, Deerfield's minister from 1732-1780, was living in Deerfield in 1746 when Indians attacked the Bars settlement south of the village street. When she gave the halter to Deerfield Academy she described it in detail, ''A Line taken from an Indian who was killed in the Bars-Fight (so called) in this town Aug. 25th 1746. It is called by the Indians the 'Captive Line.' The inside of the belt was filled with the sharp points of Hedge Hog quills and when a prisoner was led in triumph was put round his neck with one Indian forward and one behind him, each holding the line.''

   Gift of Mrs. Dorothy Ashley to Deerfield Academy Museum before 1799; transferred to PVMA in 1877.

19. BAYONET, made in France, c. 1670-1700.

This versatile bayonet was designed for use either at the end of a musket barrel or to be hand-held as a dagger. Cast-brass helmeted soldiers decorate the quillion and pommel of this rare seventeenth-century weapon. An early and undated label inside the linen sheath reads, ''This knife was taken from the hand of an Indian Chief who was killed while in (the act) of scalping a white man he had killed in one of the skirmishes between colonists and indians [*sic*] about the time of the Bloody Brook Massacre near Deerfield, Mass. by Capt. Henry Jewett, a noted indian fighter and scout of those remote days...and has descended to the present owner Mr. John F. Greene of Putnam....'' Although the bayonet is contemporary with the 1675 massacre at Bloody Brook, its Connecticut provenance casts doubt on a Deerfield association.

   Gift of Mrs. George G. Bass for her son George G. Bass, Jr., 1950.

20. TAPESTRY CUSHION COVER, made at the Sheldon family tapestry workshop, England, c. 1610-1615.

The Reverend Edward Taylor (1642-1729) brought this cushion cover with him from England in 1662, when he arrived to settle in Massachusetts. In 1671 Taylor left Cambridge to become the first minister of Westfield, Massachusetts. The Mannerist design and former vibrant colors of the cushion cover reflect seventeenth-century tastes. The donor, the Reverend John Taylor (1762-1840), was Deerfield's minister from 1787-1806 and a grandson of Edward Taylor.

Gift of the Reverend John Taylor to Deerfield Academy Museum before 1806; transferred to PVMA in 1877.

21. PLATE, tin-glazed earthenware, England, early eighteenth century.

Descended in the family of Esther Williams (1691-1751), oldest daughter of Deerfield's Reverend John Williams, tradition holds that this nine-inch delft plate was given to Esther by her father at the time of her marriage to the Reverend Joseph Meachem of Coventry, Connecticut, in 1715. Of English origin, the plate has no foot ring and is decorated under the glaze in blue. The medallion, or six-petal rosette, is reminiscent of an architectural detail or of an embroidery motif in eighteenth- and nineteenth-century needlework.

Gift of Mrs. Bessie Gamons, 1954.

22. DRUG JAR, tin-glazed earthenware, England, 1675-1775.

The donor of this delft drug jar, Catherine E. (Bardwell) Allen, niece of Mrs. E.H. Williams, inherited many items from the Ebenezer Hinsdale Williams family. This physician's drug jar and a fleam, a medical bleeding tool, given by her to Memorial Hall, perhaps originally belonged to Dr. Thomas Williams (1736-1815) of Roxbury, Massachusetts, the father of E.H. Williams. Drug jars, usually oviform in shape and used for dry medicines, were counted among the possessions of physicians. These forms, often adorned with a cartouche draped with swags and tassels, were made in England for one hundred years, beginning about 1675. Within the cartouche "P Cochlearia," the "P" indicated the form in which the drug was processed, probably pills (pilulae), which were commonly contained in these three to four inch pots. "Cochlearia" refers to the herb scurvy grass.

Gift of Mrs. Catherine E. (Bardwell) Allen, 1886.

23. PEWTER FLAGON, impressed "TL" in a heart, possibly Thomas Lupton, London, c. 1680-1700.

Inscribed "DC" on the handle, this flat-topped flagon has a history of use in the Deerfield church, founded in 1686, and was probably intended to bring unconsecrated wine to the communion table. Pewter communion vessels were often later replaced by ones of silver. The maker's mark is impressed inside the bottom.

Gift of the Deerfield Church, before 1886.

24.

24. SIDE CHAIR WITH LEATHER UPHOLSTERY, owned in the Amsden family, made in New York, 1660-1680.

Owned by John Amsden (1686-1742) of the Bars settlement in Deerfield, this chair came to Memorial Hall from the house of Samuel Allen (1702-1746), a neighbor of John Amsden. Joseph Negus Fuller (1824-1895), the donor, resided in the former Samuel Allen house. This chair form, fashionable through the seventeenth century, required the skills of three craftsmen — the turner, the joiner, and the upholsterer. Both the seat and the upper portion of the back of the Amsden chair were originally stuffed with marsh grass and covered with leather which was secured with brass tacks. Durable and handsome, leather was more costly and showy than wood or rush but less expensive than cane or a textile. The front posts are turned. The stretchers are characteristic of those on chairs made in New York: on each side are two plain rectangular stretchers, while the front and rear each have only one.

Gift of Joseph N. Fuller, 1880.

25. SIDE CHAIR, owned by the Nims family, Deerfield area, 1680-1720.

Made by a turner, this small chair appears in the 1831 inventory of Seth Nims as "one short legged chair" valued at twenty cents. It remained in the Nims home, just north of Deerfield's White Church, until it was given to Memorial Hall by Eunice Kimberly (Nims) Brown (1845-1917) in 1880 — the year the museum opened. Eunice, descendant of the original settler Godfrey Nims and last family member to live on the Nims homelot, inherited the present Nims house with its contents which had descended to her through four successive male generations. Considering this chair's long life and the heavy use given to seating furniture, repairs and missing or replaced parts are not unexpected. The upper sections of the urn and ball finials on the rear posts are missing and the legs have been shortened. The ash and maple chair was originally painted red.

Gift of Eunice K. (Nims) Brown, 1880.

25.

26. JOINED CHEST, probably Windsor, Connecticut, c. 1640-1680.

This chest descended in the Hoyt family, whose earliest known ancestor, Nicholas Hoyt, died in Windsor in 1655. His son, David Hoyt (1651-1704), was probably born in Windsor and migrated to Hatfield, Massachusetts, and then to Deerfield about 1682. It is entirely possible that David Hoyt carried the chest with him when he journeyed north from Windsor. The oak chest, which has lost its legs and its lid, remained in the Hoyt family until given to PVMA. The carving on the top and bottom rails is continued on both ends, a feature common to chests with Windsor histories.

Gift of Catherine W. Hoyt, before 1886.

27. JOINED CHEST WITH DRAWER, probably Hatfield, Massachusetts, 1695-1715.

Probably made for Rebecca Allis (b. 1683), possibly by her father, John Allis (1642-1691) of Hatfield, the "RA" chest is one of ten joined chests in Memorial Hall and survives with its original red and black paint. Rebecca Allis married Nathaniel Graves in 1702. This "Hadley Chest" (a term introduced in 1883 by a collector, Henry Wood Erving) is one of a body of furniture, including chests and boxes, made in western Massachusetts in the late seventeenth and early eighteenth centuries. Most of the carved examples were constructed of red oak and pitch or yellow pine. Drawer facades and panels were usually carved separately, the design probably laid out with a template to assure regularity. Paint, typically red and black, was often applied before the assembly of the parts, and the characteristic carving — a flat flower and leaf motif — was done after the assembly. In this example the woodworker used a gouge to highlight the recessed area of the facade decoration. The chest descended in the Graves family of Hatfield.

Gift of Chester Graves Crafts, 1887.

28. JOINED CHEST WITH TWO DRAWERS in-
itialed "SW," Hadley area, Massachusetts,
1695-1720.

The painted decoration on the "SW" chest is its
major feature. Stylized vines and a variety of
geometric shapes, achieved by the use of a com-
pass, ornament the rails, stiles, and panels of the
facade. Each of the two drawers is bordered
with blue paint, creating the illusion of two
pairs of drawers, and an initial appears on each
of the center stiles rather than within the center
panel as on most of the carved examples. The
work of a joiner, this oak and white pine chest
shares the construction techniques of carved
chests made in the comparable time period and
geographic area. Its showy decoration was probably the work of a separate craftsman.
Although two other similarly decorated examples with Hadley or Hatfield histories are
known, no information exists to point to the
person(s) who embellished them. The geometric
designs of the "SW" chest retain their integrity,
but the paint itself has been "improved." The
donor George Sheldon purchased the chest
about 1870 from Jonathan A. Saxton of Deerfield, whose wife, Miranda Wright, descended
through her mother from two related branches
of the White family of Hatfield, thus lending
credence to the tradition that the "SW" chest
came down in the White family. Miranda's
great-great grandfather, John White of Hatfield
(c. 1663-1750), was a joiner.

    Gift of George Sheldon, 1892.

29. JOINED CHEST WITH THREE DRAWERS,
owned by Sarah Hawks (1701-1783), Deerfield
area, 1710-1726.

One of two known joined and carved chests
with three drawers, this example descended in
the Hawks and the Wells families of Deerfield.
Sarah Hawks married Thomas Wells on
November 22, 1726, and according to George
Sheldon, "an oak chest and draws, part of her
outfit, is in Memorial Hall." Monogrammed
"SH," the chest retains much of its original red
and black paint.

    Gift of George Sheldon, before 1886.

30. PORTRAIT OF THE REVEREND STEPHEN WILLIAMS, (1693-1782), attributed to Joseph Badger (1708-1765), c. 1750.

Stephen Williams was the first minister of Longmeadow, Massachusetts, where his influence as a preacher from 1716-1782 was felt throughout the Connecticut River Valley. Third son of the Reverend John Williams, minister in Deerfield during the 1704 French and Indian attack, the then ten-year-old Stephen was taken captive with his family and forced to march to Canada, where he was held for more than a year. This portrait was probably painted in Boston; portraitists were not known to have worked in western Massachusetts until the late eighteenth century.

Gift of Deacon Jabez Backus Root, 1889.

31. TABLE, Deerfield, probably made by a member of the Munn family of woodworkers in Deerfield, 1740-1780.

This cherry fall leaf, or drop leaf, table was owned by the Hoyt family in the Old Indian House. The shaped skirts at each end are applied and intended to accentuate the curvature of the legs. Two of the four legs are fixed and the other two move to support the leaves. These tables conveniently seat four to six people. When not in use the relatively light-weight table can easily be folded and placed against the wall.

For three generations members of the Munn family in Deerfield were woodworkers. Benjamin Munn (1683-1774) and his son Benjamin (1708- c.1778) were carpenters; both the second Benjamin's son, Benjamin (1738-1824) and his nephew Francis C. Munn (1743-1818) were joiners.

Gift of Mrs. Catherine W. Hoyt, before 1886.

32. CUPBOARD, from the Elijah Williams house, Deerfield, c. 1760.

This architectural shell cupboard flanked the parlor fireplace in the north room of the Elijah Williams house when it was built facing Deerfield's common in 1760. Formerly believed to be the house built by the town in 1707 for Elijah's father, the Reverend John Williams (and still known locally as the John Williams House), the 1760 house was moved to the west in 1877 to make room for the new building of Dickinson High School and Deerfield Academy. The cupboard was purchased for ten dollars by PVMA. The 1920 catalogue states "this is the only article in Memorial Hall for which any money has been paid by the PVM Association." Not until the 1980s were additional objects purchased for the collection. The upper portion of this pine cupboard, with its carved scallop shell, fluted pilasters, and curvilinear shelves, was intended for display of treasured possessions, probably ceramics and glass. The lower section, designed for storage, is enclosed by two paneled doors held in place with foliated hinges fixed with rose head nails. The hardware was probably made by the Deerfield blacksmith John Partridge Bull. The red paint has been renewed, but the interior retains an old brown color and the edges of the shelves are painted green.

Another "shell cupboard" survives in Deerfield in the Thomas Dickinson house, built about 1760. Other nearly identical cupboards can be traced to Connecticut River Valley houses as far south as Middletown, Connecticut, and west as far as Ashley Falls, Massachusetts.

Museum purchase, 1879.

33. WRITING ARM WINDSOR CHAIR, made by Ebenezer Tracy (1774-1803), Lisbon, Connecticut, 1765-1790.

This high-backed writing arm Windsor, made of hickory, maple, oak, and chestnut, was once owned by the pastor of the Congregational Church of Shelburne, Massachusetts, the Reverend Theophilus Packard (1769-1855). Chairs of this type, equipped with a writing surface and storage drawers, served as desks and were often owned by lawyers and ministers, men who regularly devoted time to writing and to correspondence. A product of the shop of Colonel Ebenezer Tracy, Connecticut's most accomplished Windsor chair maker, it is branded three times under the seat: "EB: TRACY." The bulbous turnings, finely executed and of ample proportions, are complemented by a circular seat of chestnut surmounted by shaped spindles. The two drawers, one beneath the seat and the other under the large writing arm, are an added convenience and both are fitted with locks. Because of the variety of woods used in their construction, nearly all Windsor chairs were intended to be painted. This example was originally green. Windsor chair makers ideally used some unseasoned wood to insure tight joints with the result that the best of these chairs are not only handsome and comfortable, but strong as well.

Bequest of Francis J. Kellogg, 1935.

34. SIGN FOR THE EPHRAIM WELLS TAVERN, Greenfield, c. 1809-1818.

This sign once hung outside the Greenfield Meadows tavern of Ephraim Wells (1772-1818). One side shows Commander-in-Chief George Washington, the other an Indian.

Gift of Charles T. Nims, 1878.

35. ENGRAVING, "The Bloody Massacre," by Paul Revere, Boston, 1770.

This widely distributed print was influential in uniting Colonists in the spirit of rebellion against the British. The hand-colored engraving is a distorted representation of British soldiers firing upon Bostonian "Sons of Liberty." The donor's grandfather, Justin Hitchcock of Deerfield (1752-1822) served as fifer in a company of minute men.

Gift of Eunice K. (Hitchcock) Huntington, before 1886.

36. BIRCH BARK POWDER MAGAZINE, owned by John Hawks (1707-1784), c. 1740-1760, and POWDER HORN, owned by Eleizer Hawks (1717-1746), c. 1735-1746.

Lt. Colonel John Hawks was known as the "Hero of Fort Massachusetts" for his brave defense of the fort located near the present Williamstown, Massachusetts, against 700 French and Indians on August 19, 1746. Six days later, several Indians attacked the Bars settlement, south of Deerfield, where Eleizer Hawks, nephew of John, was killed while carrying this powder horn.

Powder magazine: Gift of William Guinan, before 1886. Powder horn: Gift of Colton Stebbins, 1910.

37. CHEST OF DRAWERS ON FRAME, probably made by a member of the Munn family of woodworkers in Deerfield, c. 1769.

This scallop-top chest on frame was a gift to Persis Hoyt (1747-1830) from her father, David Hoyt, at the time of her marriage to John Sheldon in Deerfield in 1769. Similar chests have descended in the families of two sisters of Persis, each with a wedding present tradition. This cherry chest retains its original finish and most of the original hardware. The central upper drawer, with a carved fan, is flanked by a pair of narrow drawers on each side, an arrangement reminiscent of some tall chests and chests-on-chests of the same period. Furniture with shaped tops, an expression of the Rococo style, represents a unique product in the Connecticut River Valley. The idea may have been developed in the Hartford, Connecticut area. The earliest documented examples are associated with nearby Wethersfield, however by the time this chest was made, cabinetmakers in towns throughout the region had adopted the style.

Gift of George Sheldon, before 1886.

38. HIGH CHEST OF DRAWERS, owned by Mary Stratton Stebbins (1749-1830) of Belchertown, Massachusetts, c. 1772.

Believed to have been part of the "wedding outfit" of Mary Stratton Stebbins of Belchertown when she married Samuel Hinsdale of Greenfield, Massachusetts, in 1772, this maple high chest conforms to the style known as Queen Anne or Rococo. A departure from the heavy joined oak chests of the late seventeenth and early eighteenth centuries, the high chest was made by a cabinet maker rather than the joiner of an earlier period, and was intended for the storage of textiles — clothing and household linens. This square-head, or flat top case of drawers, is constructed of lightweight dovetailed maple boards and displays a curvilinear skirt, delicately shaped cabriole legs, and thirteen convenient drawers.

The chest was originally grained or painted red but now has a black finish. The carved shell on the central drawer of the lower case may be original, and the pinwheel in the upper section was probably added later.

Gift of Fannie and Emily Hinsdale, 1876.

39. SIDE CHAIR, owned by the Nims family of Deerfield, 1780-1810.

The work of turners, bannister back chairs of this type were made in great numbers over a long period of time. The bannisters are split spindles rather than slats and their turnings ideally match the rear posts of the chair, as in this example. The posts are topped with attenuated spools. As in many similar Deerfield chairs, the split bannisters are reversed, placing the rounded surface against the sitter's back. The two front stretchers are modestly ornamented, while those on the side and back are plain. The arched crest with its cyma curve is finished with a beveled edge, and the chair retains an early splint seat and an old red surface. Owned in the Nims family, it was probably purchased by Seth Nims (1762-1831), and was given to Memorial Hall by a Nims descendant.

Gift of Eunice K. (Nims) Brown, 1880.

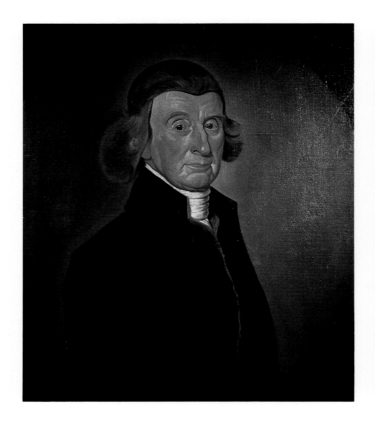 

40. PORTRAITS OF ELIJAH ARMS (1712-1802) AND NAOMI LYMAN ARMS (1739-1818), by William Jennys (active 1793-1807), Deerfield, c. 1801.

Elijah and Naomi Arms of Deerfield were painted by the itinerant artist William Jennys, who is known to have worked in New York and Connecticut before traveling north along the Connecticut River to Deerfield about 1801. Housewrights and furniture makers traveled to Deerfield and its neighboring towns from Connecticut to the south, and it is therefore not surprising that portrait painters followed the same route up the valley. These two portraits share characteristics found in other works of William Jennys: painted spandrels define the corners and the sitters' faces are brightly illuminated (casting distinct nose shadows and making shiny reflections). Over one hundred portraits by Jennys have been identified. Elijah Arms, who married Naomi Lyman of Northampton in 1774, resided in the settlement of Mill River south of Deerfield's village street.

Gifts of Philomelia Arms Williams, 1903.

41. OVERMANTEL PANEL, from the Burk Tavern, Bernardston, Massachusetts, attributed to Jared Jessup, c. 1813.

In preference to hanging a painting over his fireplace, a late-eighteenth- or early-nineteenth-century homeowner might commission a scenic landscape to be painted directly onto a chimney breast. Jared Jessup of Long Island, New York, and Richmond, Massachusetts, was probably responsible for this harbor scene as well as similar overmantel paintings in the Ryther house in Bernardston, in the Arms house in Deerfield, and in the Waid-Tinker house in Old Lyme, Connecticut. The hole in the panel was one later owner's solution to accommodate a stovepipe.

Gift of the Frizzell brothers, 1873.

42. BASKET WITH COVER, cream-colored earthenware, England, c. 1770s-1780s.

This oval ceramic basket belonged to Deerfield resident Lucy Frary (1754-1831), who married Colonel Joseph Stebbins (1749-1816) in 1774. It was inherited by their daughter, Caroline (Stebbins) Sheldon, and descended to her son, George Sheldon. The litchi nut finial on the cover is comparable to those seen on Chinese export porcelain wares. The basket has twisted handles fixed to the body with small rosettes. English creamware, produced primarily in the Staffordshire district and in the city of Leeds, began to replace delft in the mideighteenth century and remained dominant in England until the nineteenth century. Considered by some the triumph of English ceramics, creamware is light in weight, and the best examples have a good clear creamy color.

Gift of George Sheldon, 1889.

43. PORTRAIT OF RHODA WRIGHT SMITH, (1775-1818), attributed to Charles Lyman (1778-1814), Northfield, Massachusetts, 1794.

Before the Revolution, only well-to-do persons had the means to sit for a portrait. However, by the late eighteenth century, and increasingly so in the early nineteenth century, persons of more modest means, including Rhoda Smith of Northfield, were able to have their portraits painted. No longer looking to England for artistic precedents, artists with little or no training began to portray Americans less expensively and with less formality than those of preceding generations. This painting is one of the earliest surviving portraits painted in the present Franklin County. Rhoda was nineteen when her portrait was painted. When twenty-five, she attended Deerfield Academy, and in 1807 she married Henry Bardwell of Deerfield. Charles Lyman was the son of Caleb and Catherine (Swan) Lyman of Northfield.

Gift of Catherine E. (Bardwell) Allen, 1889.

44. EMBROIDERY, "The Shepherdess of the Alps" by Emily Trowbridge (1793-1872), c. 1805-1810.

Embroidery was an integral part of a young lady's education in the late eighteenth and early nineteenth centuries. Inspired by a scene from a literary work, Jean F. Marmontel's 1766 French play published in *Moral Tales*, London, 1800, Emily displayed her knowledge as well as her needlework skills in this silk embroidery. Emily Trowbridge of Deerfield married Ephraim Williams (1760-1835), also of Deerfield, in 1815; her needlework, however, relates to embroidery from Rhode Island, where she may have attended school.

Gift of Bishop John Williams, 1899.

45. SILK EMBROIDERY OF MOUNT VERNON, by Caroline Stebbins (1789-1865), Deerfield, c. 1806-1807.

The engraving of Mount Vernon by Francis Jukes is a patriotic scene copied by many New England schoolgirls in the early nineteenth century. Caroline Stebbins embroidered this version when a pupil of Jerusha Williams at Deerfield Academy. Miss Williams taught fine needlework and painting skills at the Academy between 1806 and 1812. Caroline Stebbins, of Deerfield, married Seth Sheldon in 1810.

Gift of George Sheldon, 1893.

46. WALLPAPER BOXES, Franklin County, Massachusetts, c. 1810-1845.

These boxes, made of wood or cardboard and covered with blockprinted wallpaper, were intended for the storage of bonnets and hats. Clockwise, upper left: box with parrots that belonged to Anna (Williams) Howard (1799-1822), Deerfield, c. 1818; box with hounds chasing hares, Deerfield, c. 1810-1820; box with geometric patterns, owned by Harriet A. Nash (b. 1807), Greenfield, Massachusetts, 1829-1834; box depicting the United States Capitol that once belonged to Elizabeth (Hale) Cushman (b. 1874), Bernardston, Massachusetts, 1845.

Box with parrots: Gift of Mrs. Catherine E. (Bardwell) Allen, 1882. Box with hounds: Gift of same, before 1886. Box with geometric pattern: Donor unknown. Box with Capitol: Gift of Aimee Whithead, 1921.

47. PASTEL OF JANE MARSHALL WOOD (1833-1841), by Ruth Henshaw Bascom (1772-1848), Greenfield, Massachusetts, 1836.

Ruth Bascom, of Leicester, Massachusetts, drew over 1,100 life-size profile portraits between 1819 and 1848. A minister's wife, seamstress and a milliner, as well as a pastelist, Aunt Ruth, as she was affectionately known to family and friends, traveled throughout New England drawing pastels. Her husband, the Reverend Ezekiel Bascom, was born in Greenfield and had relatives both there and in neighboring Bernardston and Gill, thus providing a wide circle of patrons for his wife in Franklin County. While visiting her husband's niece Eunice Rowena (Hosmer) Wood in Bernardston during the winter of 1836, Mrs. Bascom drew pastels of two of the Wood children, Jane and Aura, and returned a few years later to complete a portrait of their younger sister Abby Wood. All three pastels are on display in Memorial Hall.

Gift of Mrs. Edwin Day Scott, 1959.

48. SAMPLER, made by Mary Hawks (1799-1876), Deerfield, 1809.

Samplers were often sewn by girls between the ages of six and twelve as part of their primary education. Patterns were passed among families and friends, and a number of local samplers dating 1794-1816 share motifs similar to this silk on linen example by Mary Hawks. Stitched in the lower center beneath the basket of flowers is "Mary Hawks/AE 10 1809." Known throughout her adult life as "Little" Mary because of her diminutive 3' 4" height, Mary was the daughter of Zur and Martha (Arms) Hawks of Deerfield.

Gift of Miss Lucy Pratt, 1953.

49. PAINTING, "Schoolroom at the Mill and Bars: Recitation Day," attributed to James Wells Champney (1843-1903), c. 1877-1887.

At the end of a school term, parents and townspeople were invited to listen to the pupils' oral examinations, orations, and declamations. This painting is believed to be of the district schoolhouse at the Mill and Bars settlement, south of Deerfield's village street. James Wells Champney, to whom the painting has traditionally been attributed, was a painter, illustrator, pastelist, and photographer, maintaining a studio in Deerfield and in New York City.
   Gift of Stephen Maniatty, c. 1945.

50. SILHOUETTE, possibly of Abigail Whitney (1786-1833), Shelburne, Massachusetts, 1808.

This silhouette was cut from the front page of the October 3, 1808 Greenfield *Gazette*. In the early nineteenth century the silhouette became popular as an inexpensive means to record a likeness. Although tradition has identified this profile as Hannah Whitney (1788-1859) of Shelburne, recent research suggests her sister Abigail Whitney as the subject. Abigail's marriage to the Reverend Amariah Chandler of Deerfield took place on October 2, 1808, one day prior to the newspaper date.
   Gift of Mrs. Edward Decker, c. 1972.

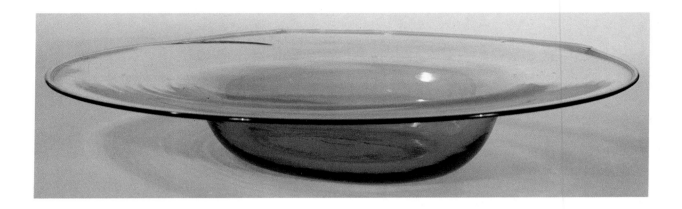

51. GLASS DISH, made at the Franklin Glass Factory, Warwick, Massachusetts, 1813-1816.

The Franklin Glass Factory was founded in 1812 when the importation of glass from England was halted by the War of 1812. The short-lived factory failed after only three years. The free-blown dish was owned by Lucy Carter of Warwick, who brought it with her when she married Dr. George Bull of Shelburne, Massachusetts, in 1838.

Gift of Julia Robbins, 1886.

52. CRUET SET, New England, c. 1815-1825.

This mahogany stand containing blown glass condiment bottles was a welcome sight on a nineteenth-century table, when the flavor of foods frequently needed to be enhanced. Blown glass bottles such as these were produced at various New England glasshouses by the nineteenth century. Ephraim and Rebecca (Jackson) Williams of Deerfield, who married in 1822, probably owned this cruet set. It descended to their granddaughter Mary Williams (Field) Fuller, also of Deerfield.

Museum purchase, 1990.

53. AMETHYST GLASS VASE, probably made at the New England Glass Company, Cambridge, Massachusetts, c. 1854.

This blown glass vase was given to Susan (Childs) Starr (1821-1900) of Deerfield by her friends and neighbors in 1854 before she moved to Laona, Illinois, with her husband, Caleb Starr, and their children.

Gift of Miss Josephine Starr, 1954.

54. GLASS MEDICINAL BOTTLES, from the nineteenth and early twentieth centuries.

Medicinal bottles contained remedies for every possible ailment and frequently had embossed descriptive titles, including the proprietor's name. From the left the bottles are labeled: "Charles Devel, Druggist, Amherst, Mass," "Mrs. Winslow's Soothing Syrup, Curtis & Perkins, Proprietors," "J.A. Darling Apothecary, Turners Falls, Mass," "Dr. Marshall's Aromatic Catarrh Snuff," "Otis Clapp & Sons. Camphour Diskoids, Boston," and "Oil Cloves for Toothache, Morse's Drug Store Geo. N. Morse, Prop., South Deerfield, Mass." These bottles are part of a collection acquired over the donor's lifetime of ninety-six years.

Gifts of Frederick R. Bridges, in memory of the Bridges family, 1985 and 1987.

55. PLATTER, pearlware, England, 1815-1835.

This platter with a transfer-printed scene of a boy piping to sheep belonged to Joanna Smith, wife of Ebenezer Hinsdale Williams, and aunt of the donor. Pearlware, a modification of the earlier cream-colored earthenware, was introduced in England in the second half of the eighteenth century when transfer-printed designs began to take the place of hand painting. The border is composed of a ring of primroses and heartsease.

Gift of Mrs. Catherine E. (Bardwell) Allen, 1889.

56. STONEWARE CHURN, "Orcutt and Wait/Whately." STONEWARE STORAGE JUG, "T. Crafts and Co./Whately/2." STONEWARE STORAGE JUG, "T. Crafts and Co./Whately/3." TWO EARTHENWARE TEAPOTS.

Production of stoneware vessels had begun in Whately, Massachusetts, by 1816. The partnership of Orcutt and Wait, active for only nine months, produced churns like the one above. Highly fired from dense white clay, brought up the Connecticut River from New Jersey, the wares are non-porous and durable, and the salt glaze made them suitable for the storage of acidic foods and liquids. The manufacture of black teapots in Whately, was introduced by Sanford S. Perry shortly before 1821 and was continued by Thomas Crafts, who also manufactured stoneware vessels, until 1832. Local deposits of manganese and galena, mixed and fired, created the black metallic lustre over the redware body. The teapots were sold locally as well as in the markets of Philadelphia and New York City.

Churn: Donor unknown. Jug: Gift of William and Suzanne Flynt, 1986. Jar with cover: Donor unknown. Teapots: Gifts of George Sheldon.

59. ALLEN SISTERS PHOTOGRAPH, "Betty at the Churn," Deerfield, 1904.

57. CHURN, (left), branded "E. Clap," owned in Deerfield's Williams family, and CHURN, (right), owned by Caroline (Stebbins) Sheldon, Deerfield, 1810.

Milk, difficult to keep, was very often consumed in the form of butter and cheese, and churns, either of wood or pottery, were common in kitchen inventories of the eighteenth and nineteenth centuries. In any region where the temperature fell below freezing, one of the late fall chores for the housewife was to churn butter for winter use or for trade. Stored between layers of salt in a cool cellar or pantry, butter could be kept for months.

    Left: Gift of Mrs. Mary Williams Fuller, 1926. Right: Gift of George Sheldon, before 1886.

58. TOASTER, America, 18th century.

This decorative and useful iron kitchen implement, probably made by a local blacksmith, was used to toast bread in front of the fire. Fleur-de-lis form the decoration on the rack portion, which pivots to enable the bread to be browned on each side.

    Gift of Joseph Robbins, before 1886.

Depicted in the Allens' kitchen is Miss Elizabeth Temple, portrayed in a domestic setting churning butter. Frances Stebbins Allen (1854-1941) and Mary Electa Allen (1858-1941) began photographing their family, neighbors, and the town of Deerfield in 1890. For the next thirty years, they recorded their community with romanticized views of the past with a high degree of technical competence and aesthetic sensitivity. Many of their original prints are preserved in the PVMA collection.

60. PORTRAITS OF PERSIS RUSSELL MONTAGUE, (1765-1851) AND WILLIAM MONTAGUE (1760-1839), by Erastus Salisbury Field (1805-1900), Sunderland, Massachusetts, c. 1836.

Born in Leverett, Massachusetts, Erastus Salisbury Field studied painting in New York in 1824 with artist and inventor Samuel Finley Breese Morse (1791-1872). The following year he commenced working as an itinerant artist in Massachusetts, where he painted sharply delineated and colorful portraits. Field was both prolific and prosperous in his painting commissions. From 1841 to 1848 he again resided in New York, and began to paint landscapes. After the 1839 invention of the daguerreotype, he worked from photographs of his subjects instead of directly from sittings, and the result was staid and uninspired portraits. For the last forty years of his career, Field concentrated on large religious and historical scenes.

William Montague and Persis Russell were married in 1786. They settled on a farm just below the Sunderland line in Hadley and had ten children. Their portraits were probably painted in commemoration of their fiftieth wedding anniversary in 1836. Personal possessions were often included in portraits, and accordingly, William holds his snuff box and cane while Persis wears a ruffled cap, a carry-over from the days when women's heads were always covered.

Gifts of Mrs. Lucinda Montague Gunn, 1934.

61.

62.

61. FIREBOARD, from the Ryther house in Bernardston, Massachusetts, attributed to Jared Jessup, c. 1813.

Fireboards customarily covered a fireplace opening during the warm months when fires were unnecessary. The artist painted this fireboard to match a painted vase of flowers on the Ryther house parlor wall. Above the fireplace in the parlor is a harbor scene reminiscent of the overmantel panel from the nearby Burk Tavern in Bernardston.
   Gift of William Ryther, 1891.

62. FIREBOARD, from the Rufus Saxton house in Deerfield, c. 1820.

Many early-nineteenth-century fireboards were decoratively painted, and the artist of the Saxton fireboard designed this trompe l'oeil view of a well equipped fireplace.
   Gift of William Saxton, before 1886.

ELECTA FIELD

TO MISSIONS

BE YE WARMED

CONWAY MASS

63. PEONY QUILT, possibly made by Fanny Wilson (1817-1907) or by her mother, Betsey (Hoyt) Wilson (1783-1860), Deerfield, 1830-1850.

Cotton piecework and applique quilts became popular in the early nineteenth century as a result of increased availability of cotton and improved technology of roller printed textiles. Birds with hearts quilted in this counterpane suggest it may have been a wedding quilt. Three of Fanny Wilson's siblings were married during the period when the quilt was worked.

Gift of Miss Fanny H. Wilson, 1905.

64. PIECEWORK QUILT SECTIONS, made by Electa Field (1794-1868), Conway, Massachusetts, c. 1825.

Four sections reading "TO MISSIONS," "ELECTA FIELD," "CONWAY MASS," and "BE YE WARMED" accompany another section stating "HOLINESS TO THE LORD I REJOICE THEREFORE THAT I HAVE CONFIDENCE IN YOU IN ALL THINGS." This unfinished quilt top is made from 5/8 inch wide cotton strips sewn with 1/8 inch wide selvedges. The intricate piecework was done by Electa Field, daughter of Solomon and Mary (Wright) Field of Conway, who married David Edson of Buckland, Massachusetts, in 1828.

Gift of Miss Elizabeth Field, 1964.

65. WEDDING GOWN, worn by Diadama (Morgan) Field (1764-1788), Northfield, Massachusetts, 1785.

This blue wool damask open robe was worn by Diadama Morgan at her marriage to Phineas Field of Northfield in 1785. The robe was worn over a petticoat or underskirt, possibly either quilted or of a compatible dress fabric. Until this century, wedding gowns were not traditionally white nor were they intended to be worn only once. Damask and other fine textiles were costly; a bride would wear her wedding dress on future formal occasions.
    Gift of Deacon Phineas Field, 1874.

66. SHIRRED RUG, depicting the Sheldon house, made by Arabella S. Sheldon (1812-1874), Deerfield, 1842.

Arabella, daughter of Seth and Caroline (Stebbins) Sheldon, lived in the Sheldon house until her marriage to Henry Wells of Shelburne, Massachusetts, in 1843, the year after the rug was completed. A shirred rug's design is created by the unfinished edges of long narrow strips of wool folded lengthwise and then sewn onto a linen backing. Also on display in Memorial Hall is a shirred rug showing the Old Indian House worked by Arabella in 1837.
    Estate of George Sheldon, 1918.

67. PAINTING OF THE OLD INDIAN HOUSE, by George Washington Mark (1795-1879), Deerfield, 1848.

The house of John Sheldon built in 1699 is renowned for having survived the 1704 French and Indian attack on Deerfield. Interest in this historic building was heightened in 1847, when its ultimate demolition was first threatened. School children, townspeople, artists, and photographers flocked to record its appearance. Among pictorial representations of the Old Indian House preserved in Memorial Hall are paintings, drawings, prints, daguerreotypes, engraved spoons, and a shirred rug. In his 1850 *Gallery Catalogue*, the artist George Washington Mark described the Old Indian House painting as "The last copy taken before it was taken down in May, 1848." Mark had settled in Greenfield, Massachuetts in 1817 and there painted houses, signs, and furniture as well as historical, religious, genre, and landscape subjects. Self-styled "Count Mark," he was regarded in the community as an eccentric.

Gift of Deerfield Academy, 1931.

68. BARGEBOARD, from the Old Indian House, Deerfield, 1699.

This scalloped bargeboard decorated the east gable of the Old Indian House. Purely ornamental, bargeboards were time-consuming to cut, and were therefore an expensive exterior feature of a dwelling. When built, Ensign John Sheldon's house was one of Deerfield's most impressive dwellings, measuring 21' x 42'. The second story projected almost two feet beyond the first, and four carved brackets gave a false impression of supporting the overhang. Three of these brackets, along with a window casing, and an interior cornice also survived the 1848 destruction of the house and are displayed in Memorial Hall.

Probably gift of Mrs. Catherine W. Hoyt, before 1886.

69. TALL CLOCK, from the Old Ware Store, Deerfield, works attributed to Eli Terry (1772-1852), Plymouth, Connecticut, c. 1806-1809, and case probably made in Franklin County, Massachusetts, c. 1820.

This clock was retrieved from the Ware Store, facing the Deerfield common, where it stood when the building was purchased by George Sheldon in 1875 and moved in 1877. Wooden clock movements produced by reputable makers were sold by peddlers. The pine case, probably made by a local woodworker for Orlando Ware (1779-1860), was painted and grained to simulate a more expensive wood. Two of the three finial plinths have been reduced and the entire case has lost some height. The pinwheel design in the skirt is one of the most distinguishing features of the decorated case.

Gift of George Sheldon, c. 1876.

70. CRADLE, made by Wyman H. Stebbins (1807-1837) for his second daughter, Frances Stebbins, Deerfield, c. 1833.

This necessary household accessory is both deep and narrow, ideal for a newborn baby in a cold New England home. The bowed sides, dovetailed to the horseshoe-shaped end boards, rest on rockers screwed to the bottom. The distinguishing feature of the pine cradle is its decoration — sponge-like black designs daubed over an orange-red background to create a simple but pleasing effect. Wyman Stebbins, a Deerfield carpenter, died at age thirty, and when his widow married Edwin Ware in 1839, Frances Stebbins was adopted by her step-father. Her half-sister was Laura (Ware) Wilkinson, the donor.

Gift of Laura W. Wilkinson, 1891.

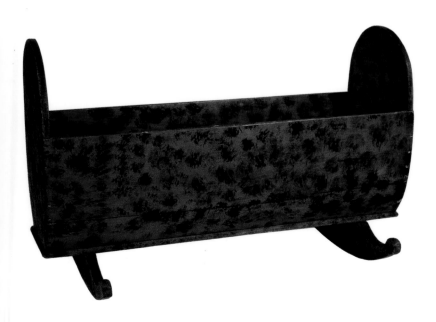

45

71. PORTRAIT OF MELINDA PROUTY LAMSON AND HER SON NATHANIEL, by Joseph Goodhue Chandler (1813-1884), Shelburne Falls, Massachusetts, 1841.

Melinda (Prouty) Lamson (1801-1874), born in West Boylston, Massachusetts, married Nathaniel Lamson, an owner of the Lamson and Goodnow Cutlery Company in Shelburne Falls, in 1833. Their only son, Nathaniel, was born in 1841. The artist Joseph G. Chandler was born in South Hadley, Massachusetts, and studied under William Collins in Albany, New York. Chandler's portraits painted during the 1840s are marked by a clarity of color and pleasant countenances. He frequently signed, dated, and identified both the name and the age of the sitter on the back of his canvas. The number of extant Franklin County portraits painted by Chandler testifies to his popularity. Certainly the Lamsons were content with his efforts, as seven portraits of family members are known.

Gift of William Lamson Warren, 1973.

72. RAG DOLL, Bangwell Putt, owned by Clarissa Field (b. 1765), Northfield, Massachusetts, c. 1770-1775.

Thought to be the oldest surviving rag doll in America, Bangwell Putt wears all the proper eighteenth-century undergarments: a linen corset with wood stays, a bodice, drawers, and a petticoat, all of linen, and a wool petticoat beneath her dress of a later period. Bangwell Putt's carefully articulated fingers suggest their importance to her owner Clarissa, who was born blind. This doll was the heroine of *The Journey of Bangwell Putt,* a children's book written by Mariana (Marian F. Curtiss) in 1945. Other dolls with fanciful names owned by Clarissa were Pingo, Palica, Kimonarro, and Ebby Puttence.

Gift of Deacon Phineas Field, 1883.

73. DOLL, LILLA, AND WATERCOLOR OF MARY ELLA CHILDS (1854-1942) HOLDING LILLA, by an unidentified artist, Deerfield, c. 1863.

Ella, the daughter of Robert and Mary (Warren) Childs, is depicted in her best dress holding her china-head doll Lilla, who wears a fashionable dress similar to Ella's.

Gifts of Miss Alice Childs, 1957.

74. BABY CARRIAGE, made by Jarvis B. Prentiss (1804-1844), Greenfield, Massachusetts, 1835.

This ornate baby carriage was built for Eliza, the infant daughter of Jarvis and Mary (Wells) Prentiss, by her father. By 1835, the manufacture of coaches and wagons was well-established in Greenfield. A knowledge of suspension systems, wheel building, upholstery, and decorative painting was needed to build a baby carriage or a coach, and Jarvis Prentiss was probably well-experienced before he constructed this fine baby carriage. Others in Greenfield also began building baby carriages or the components, and it came to be a significant local industry. In 1843 this carriage was sold to Meltiah B. and Mary S. W. Green of Worcester, Massachusetts, for their newborn son Meltiah, and in 1876 the carriage was given to Enos Wells, uncle of Eliza Prentiss. Enos Wells of Deerfield had, by that time, settled in Worcester.

Gift of Enos Wells, 1890.

75. PAINTING OF CHEAPSIDE, Greenfield, Massachusetts, 1864.

A German artist offered this painting for sale in the Greenfield *Gazette and Courier* on December 26, 1864 describing it as "a fine painting of Cheapside, taken from the south end of Congress Street." The inclusion of immigrant housing, complete with gardens and clotheslines, offers an unusual glimpse of everyday life in the nineteenth century. Situated within the boundaries of Deerfield north of the Deerfield River until 1896 when it was annexed to Greenfield, the settlement of Cheapside had been an active river port in the late eighteenth and early nineteenth centuries, but by 1864 when the painting was advertised, it had become a community largely composed of German, Irish, and Italian immigrants. The Russell Cutlery, established in 1836 on the Green River, had first attracted German settlers, and the advent of the railroad in 1846 brought Italian and Irish workers, many of whom chose to remain in Cheapside. Railroad traffic also eliminated the need for Cheapside's once active river docks and landings.

Gift of Mrs. Lucius Potter and Miss Lucia Russell, 1958.

76. PAINTING OF THE CONNECTICUT VALLEY, George Fuller (1822-1884), Deerfield, c. 1860.

Depicted in this view from Wisdom, or West Deerfield, is the easily recognizable Sugarloaf Mountain rising from the valley floor. George Fuller of Deerfield worked primarily as a portrait painter before his election as an Associate of the National Academy of Design in 1854. After years spent in Boston, New York, and in the south, Fuller returned to the family farm in the Bars section of Deerfield south of the village street in 1860 and remained there until 1875, painting only when life on the farm permitted. He then set up a studio in Boston and aligned himself with the French Barbizon School. In 1880 Fuller was elected to the Society of American Artists and enjoyed wide critical acclaim. In 1884 following his death, the Museum of Fine Arts in Boston, Massachusetts, held a memorial exhibition of 175 of George Fuller's paintings.

Museum purchase, 1987.

77. PORTRAIT OF ELIZABETH FULLER (1896-1979) by Augustus Vincent Tack (1870-1949), c. 1904.

Tack painted this portrait of his wife's niece Elizabeth early in his successful career as a portrait painter and muralist. Augustus V. Tack maintained a house and a studio in Deerfield after marrying Violet Fuller in 1900 and during his lifetime showed his paintings in over ninety exhibitions. Elizabeth, the daughter of George Spencer and Mary Williams (Field) Fuller, grew up and spent most of her life on the farm at the Bars, where her great-grandfather, Aaron Fuller, had settled in 1820. Her great-grandmother, Fanny Negus, was born into a family of artists and George Fuller (1822-1884), Elizabeth's grandfather, attained a national reputation as a painter. Elizabeth Fuller followed the tradition of generations of the Fuller and Negus families and devoted much of her life to painting, specializing in pastel portraits of children and in floral still-lifes. For many years she served as a member of the PVMA Council, or governing board, and was a founder of the Deerfield Valley Artists Association.

Gift of Mrs. Augustus V. Tack, 1957.

78. ALLEN SISTERS PHOTOGRAPH, Ladies Embroidering, Deerfield, c. 1900.

Toward the end of the nineteenth century, Americans began to look back and to take a deep interest in the Colonial past. In Deerfield early efforts to recapture and to preserve the past resulted in the founding of the Pocumtuck Valley Memorial Association in 1870, and in the opening of Memorial Hall in 1880. Generally, Victorian excesses created by advancing mechanization were shunned as admiration increased for articles crafted by hand. These sentiments guided Ellen Miller (1854-1929) and Margaret Whiting (1860-1946) when they founded the Deerfield Society of Blue and White Needlework in 1896. Trained at the New York Academy, the two friends first began to sketch patterns from old embroideries available to them at Memorial Hall and to integrate the early motifs into their own needlework designs. Within a year they had incorporated new ideas, colors, designs, dying methods, and stitches into their embroidery techniques. The village industry expanded until as many as thirty women were employed annually to embroider items to be sold at the Miller home (formerly the Nims family house) during the society's thirty-year existence. The New York *Evening Post* reported in 1897 that "the Deerfield Society of Blue and White Needlework is in perfect harmony with its environment. It is colonial and puritan, it is artistic, it is loyal to its traditions, patriotic, and there is not another like it." The Society exhibited nationally and won medals at the Pan-American Exposition in 1901 and the Panama-Pacific Exhibition in 1915.

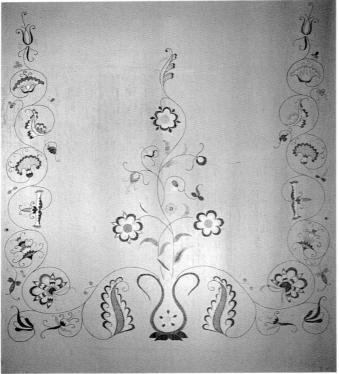

79. DOOR CURTAIN, designed by Margaret Whiting (1860-1946) and embroidered by the Deerfield Society of Blue and White Needlework, 1899.

In the late nineteenth century, curtains or portieres commonly enclosed the door opening of a room, both for physical and visual warmth. A door curtain as well as window curtains were hung in every well-appointed parlor or dining room. The Deerfield Society usually imported fine grades of hand-spun and home-woven linens from Kentucky, Georgia, and Vermont, but as in the case of this door curtain, they occasionally made use of old linen sheeting. Their embroidery threads were always also linen.

Gift of Gertrude Cochrane Smith, 1956.

80. DOILY, embroidered by the Deerfield Society of Blue and White Needlework, c. 1896-1906.

The Society's first embroideries were worked in blue on white, as suggested by its name. Doilies influenced by Colonial designs were produced in several sizes.

Donor unknown.

81. EMBROIDERY, "Sea Weed and Dragon Flies," by the Deerfield Society of Blue and White Needlework, c. 1900-1910.

Innovative designs and a variety of colors, eventually introduced into the Society's work, broadened appeal and resulted in a larger clientele. The Society sold its products from its Deerfield Shop at the Miller house, as well as by mail order, and at exhibitions. This embroidery carries the label: "The Deerfield Society of Blue and White Needlework/Embroideries of Original Design in Natural Dyes/ Established in 1896/At the Sign of the Wheel/Old Deerfield Massachusetts."

Donor unknown.

82. CENTERPIECE, "Mayflower," embroidered by the Deerfield Society of Blue and White Needlework, c. 1896-1906.

Many of the original sketches and paper patterns for the Deerfield Society's needlework survive and are preserved at Memorial Hall. This beige, blue, green, and rust colored embroidery originally sold for twenty dollars.

Gift of Mrs. Eleanor Everett, c. 1964.

83. CROSS-STITCHED EMBROIDERY, by the Deerfield Society of Blue and White Needlework, c. 1900-1920.

Within a few years after the Deerfield Society was formed, cross-stitching was introduced, and cross-stitched pieces soon comprised a large percentage of its work. Although bureau covers became one of the most prevalent forms, another included pieces intended for display on a wall as was this moral verse. At the Art Institute of Chicago's annual exhibition of handicrafts in 1903, a reviewer commented that among articles displayed by the Society "by far the most attractive things in the Deerfield case are the cross stitch pieces in color." (*House Beautiful,* October 1903).

Gift of Margery Burnham Howe, 1988.

84. BUREAU COVER, embroidered by the Deerfield Society of Blue and White Needlework, c. 1900-1920.

This embroidered bird, probably a parrot, was adapted from an eighteenth-century embroidery by Polly Wright (1752-1821) of Deerfield. The colorful interpretation of Polly's "strange ornithological specimen" makes this one of the Society's more whimsical embroideries.

Donor unknown.

85. ALLEN SISTERS PHOTOGRAPH, Pocumtuck Basket Makers, Deerfield, c. 1900.

The success of the Deerfield Society of Blue and White Needlework inspired others in Deerfield to revive a variety of crafts. The Deerfield Society of Arts and Crafts, formed in 1899, was later renamed Deerfield Industries. Madeline Yale Wynne (1847-1918) introduced raffia basketry to Deerfield and is seen here on her porch with other basketmakers. Many of the older women had witnessed or had participated in the widespread domestic industry of braiding palm leaf for bonnets, practiced in New England until about 1850, and were able to turn easily to basketry.

86. BASKETS, made by the Pocumtuck Basket Makers and by the Deerfield Basket Makers, Deerfield, c.1899-1935.

Raffia baskets made by the Pocumtuck Basket Makers, and palm leaf and reed baskets made by the Deerfield Basket Makers were produced in Deerfield homes as a cottage industry. These baskets were sold at annual exhibitions and at shops in Deerfield, where this sign once hung. Left to right: the "Witch Basket," raffia sewing basket made by Madeline Yale Wynne between 1901-1910; raffia basket made by Gertrude Porter Ashley, c. 1912; "Pansy" raffia basket made by Natalie Ashley Stebbins; palm leaf basket "Designed for a Tumbler of Flowers by Eleanor M. Arms;" reed basket with cover, c. 1910.

"Witch Basket": Gift of Elizabeth Fuller, 1976. Raffia basket: Gift of Mrs. Alice Judd, 1964. "Pansy" basket: Gift of the Misses Gladys and Mabel Brown, 1958. Palm leaf basket: Gift of Louise Perrin, 1984. Sign and reed basket: Gifts of Marion Stebbins, 1963.

87. TOOLS: auger and gouge belonged to Captain Caleb Clapp (1752-1812), Greenfield, Massachusetts, c. 1770; bevel, marked "CD," belonged to Consider Dickinson (1761-1854), Deerfield; gauge and plow, branded "I BILLINGS," belonged to Israel Jones (1787-1861), Deerfield and Wisdom (West Deerfield).

Not all woodworking tools were owned by carpenters and cabinetmakers. Neither Captain Clapp nor Consider Dickinson was a woodworker by trade. Clapp, a Revolutionary War soldier, was a well-known merchant in Greenfield and "Uncle Sid" Dickinson, who also served in the Revolution, spent some years as a fur trader in Canada. Israel Jones, who owned the gauge and the plow, made his living as a carpenter in the early nineteenth century.

Auger and gouge: Gift of Colonel Thomas Ripley, before 1886. Bevel: Gift of Justin B. Hitchcock, 1881. Gauge and plow: Gift of Mrs. Margaret Jones, 1904.

88. BROOM MACHINE, Gill, Massachusetts, c. 1840-1860, ink drawing by J. Ritchie Garrison, 1985.

Broom corn, first raised in the Connecticut River Valley about 1780, had become a staple crop by 1825. Most farmers who raised broom corn also had shops for producing the finished brooms. Albert Smith of Gill owned and used this machine now in Memorial Hall. Wire for tying came from the mills in Hadley, and the towns of Ashfield and Colrain supplied handles for the brooms, which were sold all over the country. By 1850, western prairie farmers had begun raising broom corn, and it proved to be a better product than that grown in New England. There has been little broom corn raised in the Deerfield area since 1855.

Gift of Albert Smith, 1903.

89. PATENT MODEL OF A PLOW, made by Dexter Pierce (1806-1860), Montague, Massachusetts.

Many Franklin County families have been involved in agriculture, and farming tools form an important part of the collection in Memorial Hall. This patent plow model, only eight and one-half inches long, has wooden handles and a brass plowshare reinforced with iron.

Gift of Mr. and Mrs. Edward Bartlett Wirt, 1977.

90. IRON TRAP, America, c. 1780-1820.

Made of heavy wrought iron bars and fitted with a spring mechanism and a link chain, traps were among the more complicated items made by the blacksmith. This example, with its flat-edged jaws, was probably designed to catch fur-bearing animals, possibly beavers, since it lacks the sharp iron teeth integral to the devices used to entrap wolves and bears. An early label states the trap was found on Hoosac Mountain about 1824 by Turner Potter and his father of Greenfield.

Gift of the Potter estate, 1920.

Back cover: DOLL HOUSE SIGN, painted by Dorothea Hyde Allen, Deerfield, 1923.

The "Doll House" was a tearoom and shop operated by Matilda Hyde on Memorial Street in Deerfield beginning in 1923. The sign was attached to a tree in front of the house.
  Gift of Frederick Hyde, 1981.